POWER OF INTERCESSION

Standing on God's Word through Spiritual Warfare, Discernment, and Integrity to Release Blessings

DR JACQUELINE N SAMUELS

Power of Intercession

COPYRIGHT

Copyright © 2023 **POWER OF INTERCESSION**
Standing on God's Word through Spiritual Warfare, Discernment, and Integrity to Release Blessings
by DR JACQUELINE N SAMUELS

All rights reserved.

Unless otherwise noted, all scriptures are from the NEW KING JAMES VERSION®. Copyright© 1982 by Thomas Nelson, Inc. Used by permission. All rights reserved.

Other books by the Author are available at:
https://www.amazon.com/author/jacquelinensamuels

UK: https://tinyurl.com/AuthorJNSamuelsUK

Join us for weekly prayer, thanksgiving, and worship at Supreme Global Outreach:

FB: https://tinyurl.com/SupremeGlobalOutreachFB
IG: https://www.instagram.com/supremeglobaloutreach/
TikTok: https://www.tiktok.com/@supremeglobaloutr

Training courses and products are available at:
https://serve-and-thrive-academy.thinkific.com/

Amazon ISBN: **9798858994800**

DEDICATION

I dedicate this book to every child of God who is seeking the heart and will of the Father through prayer and supplication. As you intercede for others may your cup overflow with the grace to push through in the Secret Place with ever-deepening faith and endurance. Rest assured that God hears every prayer, sees every tear, and is committed to honouring His Word to His children.

I encourage you to seek the LORD's face as you read and apply the life-changing nuggets shared in ***Power of Intercession: Standing on God's Word through Spiritual Warfare, Discernment, and Integrity to Release Blessings***.

May the Way Maker and Promise Keeper faithfully answer you and grant you victory on every side as you stand in the gap for others who need breakthroughs. In the Matchless Name of Jesus.

CONTENT

COPYRIGHT	iii
DEDICATION	iv
FOREWORD	vii
ACKNOWLEDGMENTS	ix
INTRODUCTION	xii
Chapter One: UNDERSTANDING PRAYER AND INTERCESSION	1
The Lord's Prayer	2
What is Intercession?	3
Why Pray?	4
Chapter Two: PURPOSE OF INTERCESSORY PRAYER	6
Consequences of Prayerlessness	9
Chapter Three: POWER OF PRAYER MANAGEMENT	14
Working Full-time? Prayer Management Tips	15
Chapter Four: INTERCESSION, ANSWERED PRAYERS	20
How God answered Hannah's Prayers	21
How Often Should Christians Intercede?	26
Why Intercede for Others	30
Guide to Meditating on God's Word	33
Commitment in Intercession	37
Chapter Five: TIME MANAGEMENT IN PRAYER	41
Time Management Tips for Intercession	42
The Power of Intercession to Build Faith	45
Scriptures to Grow Faith with Intercession	46
Chapter Six: POWER OF SPIRITUAL WARFARE	49

Understanding Spiritual Warfare	50
Examples of Spiritual Warfare	57
Intercessory Prayers for Spiritual Warfare	60
Chapter Seven: POWER OF SPIRITUAL DISCERNMENT	63
What is Spiritual Discernment?	64
Spiritual Alertness for Effective Prayer	65
Discernment: Responding to God's Word	69
Discernment: Interpreting God's Word	73
Verses on the Spirit of Discernment	77
Intercessory Prayers for Spiritual Discernment	80
Chapter Eight: POWER OF SPIRITUAL INTEGRITY	83
Develop Spiritual Integrity for Godly Purpose	87
Verses Celebrating Integrity	90
Intercessory Prayers for Spiritual Integrity	92
Conclusion	96
About the Author	100
Connect with the Author	101

FOREWORD

There is serious **Power in Intercession**. At an early age my mother taught me the importance of spending quality time with God. As a result, today my life has been transformed by the *Power of Prayer and Intercession*.

In 2019 the Holy Spirit impressed upon my heart to start *Divine Chanan Global Outreach (now Supreme Global Outreach)*, a platform whose vision is to connect all God's children in prayer and intercession. This turned out to be a Divine connection with author Dr Jacqueline Samuels with whom we connected during our first meeting.

Immediately her musical gifting drew us together spiritually. When I started ministering in worship, discerning that the band accompanying our worship session was not familiar with the song, Dr Jackie instantly rose from her seat and made her way to the piano and picked up the key (F Major) effortlessly.

Since that prophetic timely encounter, Dr Jackie has become a close friend, prayer warrior and has led many intercessory sessions in our SGO outreach programs. I have had the honour of witnessing Dr Jackie's spiritual growth and boldness through her constant worship and thanksgiving which encourages many believers.

The author is an ordained Pastor and Global Worship lead in SGO. We often travel locally and globally to share the love and redeeming power of Christ on various platforms. This is a testament of how the grace of God works when we walk in alignment to His leading and timing!

The LORD has enabled Dr Jackie and I to publish some prayer books arising from our training for righteousness sessions in *Supreme Global Outreach*, to the glory of God. This new book will be a welcome addition to the spiritual destiny of every believer by God's grace.

Power of Intercession outlines the Purpose of Prayer and Intercession, how to manage time for committed prayer, an essential toolkit for every busy person seeing to develop a closer relationship with the Holy Spirit. Moreover, the book addresses three key areas of intercession: *The Power of Spiritual Warfare, Spiritual Discernment, and Spiritual Integrity* without which our prayers can go astray.

Backed by numerous Biblical references, prayer points for various types of intercession, and interactive reflections, **Power of Intercession: Standing on God's Word through Spiritual Warfare, Discernment, and Integrity to Release Blessings** is a must-have tool for every Minister of the Word, Bible Scholar, Prayer Warrior, Intercessor, Sunday School Teacher, Youth Leader, Parent and Guardian seeking to nurture spiritual well-being and growth in your prayer life.

I am honoured to wholeheartedly endorse this spiritually nourishing book. Your life will never remain the same as you read and apply the secrets revealed within, in the Mighty Name of Jesus.

Chaplain Elizabeth Simuchimba
President/Founder of *Supreme Global Outreach*
Author, Mentor, Wife, Mother, Intercessor
https://amazon.com/author/chaplain-liz-simuchimba
https://tinyurl.com/30PillarsGodlyCharacter
https://tinyurl.com/SupremeGlobaloutreachIG
FB: https://tinyurl.com/SupremeGlobalOutreachFB
TikTok: https://www.tiktok.com/@supremeglobaloutr

ACKNOWLEDGMENTS

Almighty God, my Creator; Holy Spirit, my Comforter; Lord Jesus my Redeemer and Faithful Friend: Thank You for loving me, drawing me close to You and teaching me how to pray. *In You I live, breathe, and have my being.* My life and times are in Your hands of protection.

Sincere gratitude goes to the many **mentors** who have through the years taught me the value of *praying without ceasing*. While it is not possible to mention everyone who has played a role in my spiritual growth, I wish to mention the following role models who by example have inspired my journey, and continually spoken life to me.

My late mother, **Mrs Leah Wanjiru Muuya**: Thank you for being the prayerful pillar that upheld me through my youthful seasons of deep testing. Your bold worship and *'God can and will do it for me'* attitude through life's storms encouraged my vocal gift to rise and praise the LORD our Deliverer and Strength. I honour the resilience God placed in your life, Mom. Till we meet again, keep your praise fire burning in the LORD's Presence.

Mrs Annie Wangui Mwangi: You have been my long season destiny helper, prayerfully guiding my spiritual growth since childhood, youth and into motherhood. You have taught me to stand in faith and watch God fight my battles. God bless your diligence to nurture every birth child and spiritual child He has brought your way. I love and honour you, Mom.

Chaplain Elizabeth Simuchimba: Thank you my spiritual destiny helper and prayer mentor for teaching me the value and power of remaining connected to the Vine through corporate worship and intercession. As you develop leaders and nurture prayer warriors in *Supreme Global Outreach*, your life of intercession is drawing souls to Christ. I honour your prophetic, worship and deliverance ministry gifts articulated in our continuous fellowship. May the Holy Spirit refuel you to fulfil purpose in your generation and beyond.

To my family, **Reverend Dr Peter Samuels, Edy and Jonathan**: Thank you for graciously releasing me to tap into the grace bestowed upon me to intercede for our generations in these end times. I pray the LORD will keep you all aligned in His purpose for your lives and shine His glorious Light upon your paths. May He satisfy you with long, healthy, fulfilled lives, grant you endless victory with joy overflowing. I love and honour you all.

To all who have walked through spiritual growth with me: **students, clients, worship teammates, pastors, spiritual leaders**, **encouragers**, **SGO family**: Thank you. Keep your light shining as you fulfil your God-given destinies. Our Rewarder is pleased to energize us and refuel our spiritual tanks for His glory and honour.

Let us all run the race with endurance, humility, grace and ever-growing faith, for the LORD is faithful. He provides every tool we need for every purpose in His timing. Gratefully in His service,

Pastor Dr Jacqueline N Samuels
Supreme Global Outreach Worship Coordinator; Author, Publishing Coach, Editor, Graphic Designer
https://www.amazon.com/author/jacquelinensamuels

Bible Verse

Hebrews 4:16 (NKJV)

Let us therefore come boldly to the throne of grace, that we may obtain mercy and find grace to help in time of need.

INTRODUCTION

Bible Verse
1 Thessalonians 5:16-18 (NKJV)

Rejoice always, pray without ceasing, in everything give thanks; for this is the will of God in Christ Jesus for you.

Prayer is a form of worship to our Creator.
God instructs us in 1 Thessalonians 5:16-18 to
1) **Rejoice always**
2) **pray without ceasing** and
3) **in everything give thanks; for this is the will of God in Christ Jesus for you.**

Intercession involves releasing prayers that move God's heart and manifest His blessings. Galatians 6:10 exhorts us: *Therefore, as we have opportunity, let us do good to all, especially to those who are of the household of faith.*

Let us determine to support one another in prayer and supplication for this pleases our Heavenly Father. As our prayers and intercession go up His glory will manifest in and among us and our loved ones.

Our homes, families, church, and neighbourhood communities will be blessed, and we will see our children and upcoming generations grow in the knowledge of love of God through Christ Jesus.

Prayer is our spiritual weapon to pull down strongholds, equip the saints through spiritual discernment and integrity in purpose and commitment. We are each other's destiny helpers through our prayerful lifestyles individually and corporately. As Christ's ambassadors therefore, *let us approach the Throne of Grace with boldness* and obtain mercy and grace in times of need (Hebrews 4:16).

The Word recognizes our sinful condition (4:11-13).
Let us therefore be diligent to enter that rest, lest anyone fall according to the same example of disobedience. **For the word of God is living and powerful, and sharper than any two-edged sword, piercing even to the division of soul and spirit, and of joints and marrow, and is a discerner of the thoughts and intents of the heart.** *And there is no creature hidden from His sight, but all things are naked and open to the eyes of Him to whom we must give account.*

Every time we come together in prayer we connect with our Compassionate High Priest: Jesus Christ who is touched by the feeling of our infirmity. Further,
Seeing then that we have a great High Priest who has passed through the heavens, Jesus the Son of God, let us hold fast our confession. For we do not have a High Priest who cannot sympathize with our weaknesses, but was in all points tempted as we are, yet without sin. **Let us therefore come boldly to the throne of grace, that we may obtain mercy and find grace to help in time of need.**

It is for this purpose that the Holy Spirit breathed the words in this book to me: **to help every believer in and follower of Christ Jesus to come to a place of prayer, humbly seek His Word and heart, and deliver prayers of intercession for His children globally.**

In these end times we need to hold fast to our confession of faith more than ever. Praying for others and ourselves is a serious instruction that requires diligence, consistency, integrity and above all faith and humility.

POWER of INTERCESSION addresses the following:
- What is the Purpose of Prayer?
- Why Intercessory Prayers?
- What are the Consequences of Prayerlessness?
- How to Manage Time for Committed Prayer
- The Power of Spiritual Warfare
- The Power of Spiritual Discernment
- The Power of Spiritual Integrity

Scriptural references, prayer points, interactive reflections and opportunities for personal study are also provided as essential tools to empower your prayer life.

As you prepare to soak in the gems delivered in this Holy Spirit inspired book and pray the Word of God from the Holy Bible (New King James Version), open your heart and allow the Holy Spirit to minister His abounding Truth and Grace for the intercessory mission He has called us to.
I pray for Divine revelation as the LORD reveals His secrets and answers you through His dependable Word, in the Matchless Name of Jesus. In His service,
Pastor Dr Jacqueline N Samuels
Award winning Educator, Author, Publisher, Songwriter
https://www.amazon.com/author/jacquelinensamuels

Chapter One: UNDERSTANDING PRAYER AND INTERCESSION

Bible Verse

Luke 18:1 (NKJV)

Then He spoke a parable to them, that men always ought to pray and not lose heart.

Then He spoke a parable to them, that men always ought to pray and not lose heart. (Luke 18:1)

Jesus gave us the perfect model for prayer that glorifies our Heavenly Father in The Lord's Prayer. By His Own example in Matthew 6:9-14 Christ taught us the format of prayer.

Before we ask God for anything, we need to first approach Him with humility and recognize His Authority.

The Lord's Prayer

Bible Verse

Matthew 6:9-14 (NKJV)

9 In this manner, therefore, pray:
Our Father in heaven,
Hallowed be Your Name.
10 Your kingdom come. Your will be done
On earth as it is in heaven.
11 Give us this day our daily bread.
12 And forgive us our debts, as we
forgive our debtors.
13 And do not lead us into temptation,
but deliver us from the evil one.
For Yours is the kingdom and the power
and the glory forever. Amen.
14 "For if you forgive men their
trespasses, your heavenly Father will also
forgive you.

What is Intercession?

Intercession is a form of prayer in which one person prays on behalf of another, bringing their needs, concerns, and requests before God. It involves standing in the gap for others, lifting their needs to God and seeking His intervention, guidance, and blessings for their lives. Intercession is rooted in the belief that God listens to the prayers of His people and responds to their petitions.

Who Should Pray?
All believers are encouraged to engage in intercessory prayer. Intercessory prayer is not limited to a specific group or role within the church; rather, it's a responsibility and privilege that all Christians can participate in. Intercession is a way to express love, care, and solidarity within the Christian community.

When Should We Pray?
Intercessory prayer can be offered at any time. It's not restricted to a specific time of day or circumstance. However, there are various occasions that may prompt intercessory prayer, including:

- When someone is going through a challenging time or facing a crisis.
- When someone is sick or in need of healing.
- When someone is making important decisions.
- When seeking God's guidance and direction for others.
- During times of celebration, to give thanks for blessings.
- Regularly, as part of an ongoing commitment to pray for others.

Why Pray?

Do you remember the uplifting chorus that encouraged us to release worry and embrace prayer titled, *Why worry when you can pray*? When we trust Jesus with everyday decisions and experiences, we empower our faith muscles so that when trials come upon us, we can stand.

The popular 'fish story' of Jonah and the Whale recorded in the Book of Jonah chapter 2 records how he prayed after disobeying God's command to go to Nineveh and warn the inhabitants to repent or face God's wrath. Jonah's prayer in the belly of the great fish is a significant moment that reflects his acknowledgment of God's Sovereignty along with his repentance and plea for deliverance.

Then Jonah prayed to the Lord his God from the fish's belly. And he said: **"I cried out to the Lord because of my affliction, and He answered me. "Out of the belly of Sheol I cried, and You heard my voice.** *For You cast me into the deep, into the heart of the seas, and the floods surrounded me; all Your billows and Your waves passed over me. Then I said, 'I have been cast out of Your sight; yet I will look again toward Your holy temple.' The waters surrounded me, even to my soul; the deep closed around me; weeds were wrapped around my head. I went down to the moorings of the mountains; the earth with its bars closed behind me forever; yet You have brought up my life from the pit, O Lord, my God. "When my soul fainted within me, I remembered the Lord; and my prayer went up to You, into Your holy temple. "Those who regard worthless idols forsake their own Mercy.*

But I will sacrifice to You with the voice of thanksgiving; I will pay what I have vowed. Salvation is of the Lord." So the Lord spoke to the fish, and it vomited Jonah onto dry land. (Jonah 2:1-10; emphasis mine)

In this prayer, Jonah acknowledges his dire circumstances, his realization of being cast away from God's presence, and the distress he faces. He expresses gratitude for God's mercy and deliverance, even during his ordeal. In the prayer we see Jonah's shift from rebellion to surrender and a renewed commitment to worship and obedience.

God's response to Jonah's prayer is evident in verse 10: *So the Lord spoke to the fish, and it vomited Jonah onto dry land.* This shows God's mercy and willingness to respond to repentance and sincere prayers, as Jonah is given a second chance to fulfill his mission of preaching to the city of Nineveh.

Jonah's prayer serves as a powerful reminder of God's Sovereignty, His willingness to forgive and restore us, and the importance of turning to Him when we face trouble.

 ***Action steps:***

What challenge are you facing right now?
Trust God to deliver you as He did for Jonah when he prayed: *But I will sacrifice to You with the voice of thanksgiving; I will pay what I have vowed. Salvation is of the Lord.*

May the Almighty LORD who hears our secret cries answer you quickly. Thank God for every answered prayer.

Chapter Two: PURPOSE OF INTERCESSORY PRAYER

What is the Purpose of Intercessory Prayer?

Every believer in Christ needs to fuel their spiritual growth through prayers, regardless of how long they have been born again. Believers who have given their hearts to God and asked Him to forgive their sins have the advantage of *dwelling in the Secret Place of the Most High and abiding in the shadow of the Almighty* (Psalm 91:1-2).

Intercession is a powerful and meaningful form of prayer that allows believers to stand in the gap for others, seeking God's intervention and blessings in their lives.

There are several reasons why intercessory prayer is important:

Obeying Christ's Commands: Jesus taught about loving one another and supporting fellow believers. Intercession fulfills His command to care for others.

Expressing Love and Unity: Intercessory prayer demonstrates love, compassion, and unity within the body of Christ, strengthening the bonds of the community.

Seeking God's Will: By interceding, believers seek to align their prayers with God's will, asking for His plans and purposes to be fulfilled.

Bringing Needs to God: Intercession acknowledges human limitations and places trust in God's unlimited power and wisdom to address various needs.

Strengthening Faith: Intercessory prayer can uplift and strengthen the faith of others, reminding them of God's presence and care.

Promoting Healing and Restoration: Intercession contributes to spiritual, emotional, and physical healing and restoration.

Spiritual Warfare: Intercession engages in spiritual battles, seeking God's protection and victory over challenges and difficulties.

Fostering Gratitude: Seeing prayers answered through intercession fosters gratitude and encourages believers to give thanks to God.

Reflecting Christ's Character: Intercession reflects Christ's compassionate and merciful character as He intercedes on behalf of His followers.

Intercession is an expression of love, unity, and faith within the Christian community and a way to participate in God's work in the world.

Next up, let's examine:

What are the consequences of prayerlessness?

How can we reignite our prayer lives?

Consequences of Prayerlessness

Bible Verse

Ephesians 6:18 (NKJV)

Praying always with all prayer and supplication in the Spirit, being watchful to this end with all perseverance and supplication for all the saints.

Prayer should be the lifestyle of every child of God. It is for our own good and the good of all who connect with us as part of the Body of Christ. Our prayers bear fruit as we apply the principles our Heavenly Father has revealed to us through His Word.

Ephesians 6:18 encourages us to commit to *Praying always with all prayer and supplication in the Spirit, being watchful to this end with all perseverance and supplication for all the saints*. We do well to follow this instruction for spiritual growth and nourishment.

What happens when a Christian doesn't pray?

When a believer in Christ doesn't engage in prayer, several potential outcomes and effects can arise. However, it is important to note that these outcomes can vary based on individual circumstances, personal relationship with God, and the reasons behind not praying. Here are a few possible consequences:

Spiritual Neglect: Prayer is a vital means of communication with God. Not praying can lead to a sense of spiritual neglect or distance from God. Just as any relationship suffers without communication, the relationship with God can weaken when prayer is absent.

Weak Spiritual Growth: Prayer is a key component of spiritual growth. Without regular communication with God, believers might struggle to understand His will, receive guidance, and experience transformative growth in their faith.

Lack of Intimacy with God: Prayer deepens intimacy with God. Neglecting prayer can result in a lack of closeness and intimacy with Him, leading to a less fulfilling spiritual life.

Missed Opportunities for Guidance: Prayer is a way to seek God's guidance and wisdom. Not praying means missing out on the insights and direction that God may want to provide.

Inability to Overcome Temptations: Prayer is a source of strength to resist temptations. Without regular prayer, believers might struggle more with overcoming sinful habits and temptations.

Stress and Anxiety: Prayer is a means to cast anxieties and worries onto God. Not praying can contribute to heightened stress, anxiety, and a sense of trying to handle challenges on one's own.

Loss of Connection to the Body of Christ: When believers don't pray, they may miss opportunities to intercede for others and to be supported by the prayers of fellow believers, weakening the sense of connection within the body of Christ.

Missed Fellowship with God: Prayer is a way to fellowship with God and experience His presence. Neglecting prayer can lead to a lack of awareness of God's nearness and active involvement in one's life.

Lack of Thankfulness: Prayer includes expressions of thanksgiving and gratitude. Not praying can result in a failure to acknowledge and appreciate God's blessings.

Potential for Backsliding: Consistent neglect of prayer can lead to spiritual complacency and drifting away from a vibrant relationship with God, potentially leading to backsliding or a lukewarm faith.

It is worth recognizing that while prayer is crucial for spiritual growth and well-being, God's love and grace are not contingent solely on our prayers. Let us thank God who remains faithful even when we falter in our prayer life.

If someone finds themselves not praying, it provides an opportunity for reflection, repentance, and a renewed commitment to fostering a vibrant prayer life to deepen their relationship with God.

 **Action steps:**

Do you know someone who is struggling with prayer?
Yes / No

What suggestions can you give them to help them identify possible challenges?

What encouragement would you offer them based on your personal experience of prayer and what you have discovered about the benefits of prayer?

Bible Verse

1 Timothy 2:1-6 (NKJV)

Therefore I exhort first of all that supplications, prayers, intercessions, and giving of thanks be made for all men, for kings and all who are in authority, that we may lead a quiet and peaceable life in all godliness and reverence. For this is good and acceptable in the sight of God our Savior, who desires all men to be saved and to come to the knowledge of the truth. For there is one God and one Mediator between God and men, the Man Christ Jesus, who gave Himself a ransom for all, to be testified in due time.

Chapter Three: POWER OF PRAYER MANAGEMENT

Working Full-time? Prayer Management Tips

Since prayer is not an option for believers, we need to find ways of making time to meet with God and receive timely instruction from the Holy Spirit. 1 Timothy 2:1-6 exhorts us to pray for all men, regardless of their position in life.

Therefore I exhort first of all that supplications, prayers, intercessions, and giving of thanks be made for all men, for kings and all who are in authority, that we may lead a quiet and peaceable life in all godliness and reverence. For this is good and acceptable in the sight of God our Savior, who desires all men to be saved and to come to the knowledge of the truth. For there is one God and one Mediator between God and men, the Man Christ Jesus, who gave Himself a ransom for all, to be testified in due time. (1 Timothy 2:1-6)

The above list is enough to get the mind reeling. You might be wondering at this point:

Where exactly will I get the time to pray for my family, colleagues, friends, church, and ministry members, in addition to praying for our leaders and strangers?

I understand; finding time to commit to prayer is not easy. As you embark on this journey, keep in mind that you are going on a spiritual mission and your *spiritual Tour Guide* will be your ever-present Helper. You have the Holy Spirit's backing; strength will rise as you wait patiently upon the LORD.

Managing prayer time for individuals who work full-time and those called into full-time ministry can be a challenge, but with intentional planning and dedication, it's possible to maintain a rich prayer life. Here are some tips for managing prayer time effectively:

For Individuals Working Full Time:

Morning Devotion: Begin your day with a short time of devotion, including reading Scripture and offering prayers of gratitude and surrender.

Lunch Break: Utilize your lunch break for a moment of prayer and reflection. This can help refresh your spirit during the workday.

Prayer Walks: Consider taking short prayer walks during breaks or after work, using the time to connect with God and pray for various needs.

Evening Reflection: Set aside time in the evening for more in-depth prayer and reflection. This can be a time to intercede for others, seek guidance, and express personal needs.

Weekend Retreats: Plan occasional weekend retreats to spend extended time in prayer, study, and seeking God's presence. This can be especially beneficial for spiritual renewal.

Prayer:
Father, renew my strength today in the Matchless Name of Jesus, Amen.

For Individuals in Full-Time Ministry:

Structured Prayer Time: Incorporate structured prayer times into your ministry schedule. Allocate specific times for personal devotion, intercession, and seeking God's guidance.

Integrate Prayer into Ministry Activities: Embed prayer into ministry activities, such as staff meetings, worship services, and outreach events. Prioritize seeking God's wisdom and direction.

Pray with Others: Engage in corporate prayer with your ministry team and community. Praying together fosters unity and shared vision.

Balancing Ministry and Devotion: While ministry is important, don't neglect your personal devotion. Ensure that you're nourishing your own relationship with God as you pour into others.

Seasons of Rest: Recognize the need for rest and retreat. Schedule times for personal retreats to recharge and deepen your connection with God.

Delegate and Prioritize: Delegate tasks when possible and prioritize your time. Effective time management allows for both ministry responsibilities and personal spiritual growth.

Guard Your Prayer Time: Protect your prayer time from unnecessary interruptions. Communicate your need for focused prayer to those around you.

Adapt as Needed: Be flexible in your approach to prayer. Ministry demands may vary, so adjust your prayer routine to accommodate changing circumstances.

Remember that prayer is a vital aspect of both personal growth and effective ministry. Whether you work part-time, full-time or serve in full-time ministry, cultivating a consistent prayer life requires intentionality, discipline, and a heart that seeks to connect with God regularly.

Prayer:
Dear LORD, please grant me the grace to value and protect my prayer time. I realize it is important to spend regular time in Your Presence and allow You to lead me in the purpose to which You have called me. In Jesus' Mighty Name, Amen.

Bible Verse

Proverbs 3:5-6 (NKJV)

Trust in the Lord with all your heart,
And lean not on your own
understanding;
In all your ways acknowledge Him,
And He shall direct your paths.

Chapter Four: INTERCESSION, ANSWERED PRAYERS

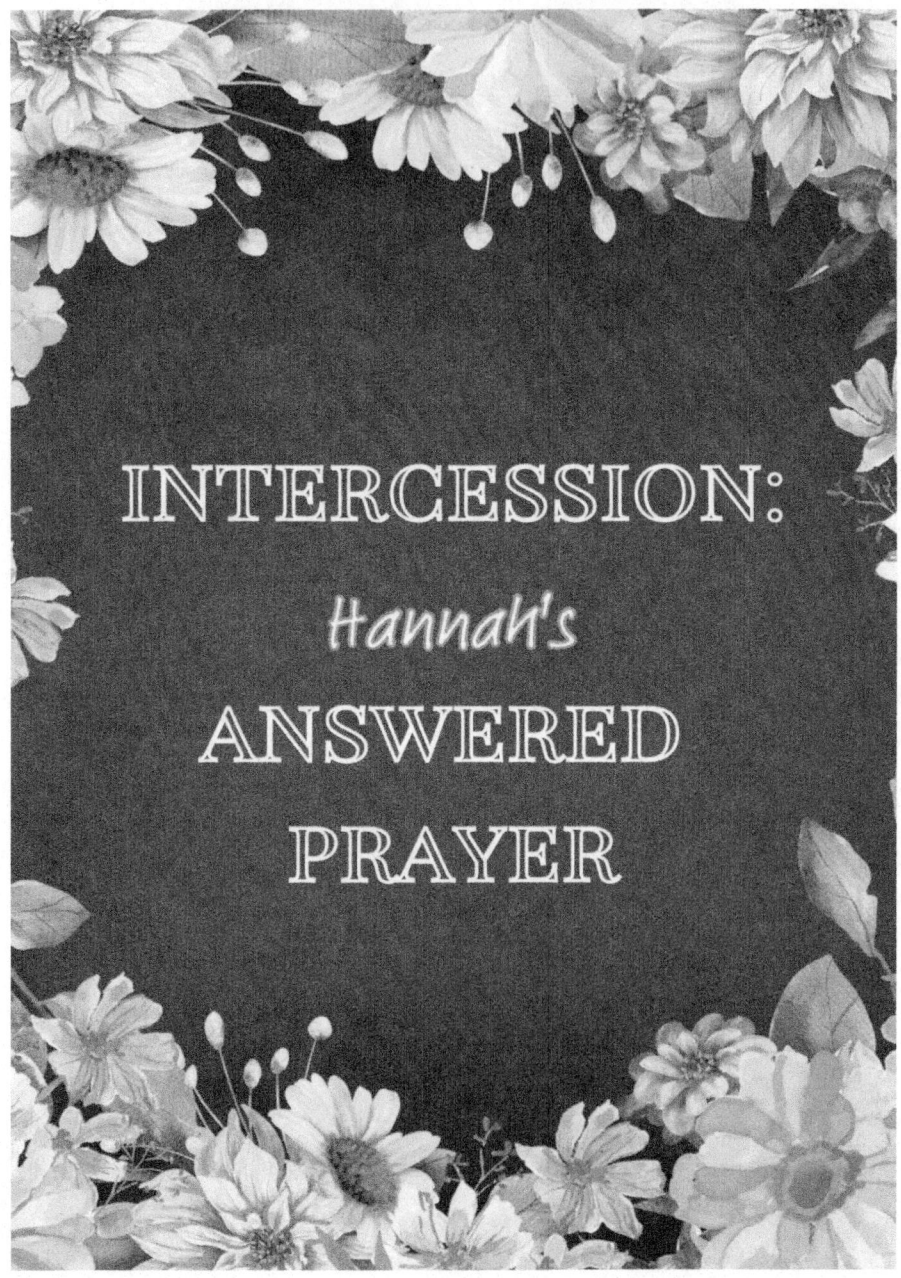

How God answered Hannah's Prayers

You might have heard of people who pray 24/7. Monks, nuns and others who have given their lives to serve the LORD in His sanctuary may often seem to have more time to commit to prayer than everyone else.

The Bible shares many stories of people who pressed into the Secret Place to petition God in prayer.

In the Old Testament, Eli and Samuel were both prophets in Israel. Eli served in the temple while Samuel served in the field; both were in full-time ministry. Both prayed and received answers from God.

Samuel was charged with the momentous task of finding and anointing the first king of Israel: David. Eli's ministry touched many people's lives including those who came to pray in the temple like Hannah.

Elkanah's wife, Hannah, was barren (1 Samuel 1:1-16). She went to the temple to worship and petition God to grant her the fruit of the womb after enduring many years of taunting by her co-wife Peninah. I believe that wasn't the first time Hannah had sought God about her predicament. Her husband Elkanah, who loved her, could not understand why she was downcast (v8).

Then Elkanah her husband said to her, **"Hannah, why do you weep? Why do you not eat? And why is your heart grieved? Am I not better to you than ten sons?"**

The family had travelled to Shiloh to worship God. Elkanah demonstrated his special favour to Hannah: *But to Hannah he would give a double portion, for he loved Hannah, although the Lord had closed her womb* (v5).

Hannah presented her grief before the LORD (v9-16):

So Hannah arose after they had finished eating and drinking in Shiloh. Now Eli the priest was sitting on the seat by the doorpost of the tabernacle of the Lord. And she was in bitterness of soul, and prayed to the Lord and wept in anguish. Then she made a vow and said, **"O Lord of hosts, if You will indeed look on the affliction of Your maidservant and remember me, and not forget Your maidservant, but will give Your maidservant a male child, then I will give him to the Lord all the days of his life, and no razor shall come upon his head."**

Meanwhile, Eli misinterpreted Hannah's petition, wrongly imagining she was drunk with wine (v12-14):

And it happened, as she continued praying before the Lord, that Eli watched her mouth. Now Hannah spoke in her heart; only her lips moved, but her voice was not heard. Therefore Eli thought she was drunk. So Eli said to her, "How long will you be drunk? Put your wine away from you!"

In verses 15-26 Hannah set the record straight. Her boldness shone through, and she was instantly rewarded for it. Do not be afraid to speak up for righteousness (with wisdom) if someone wrongly accuses you when you have been interceding for a matter close to your heart. Let God show up for you. Sometimes the result of your boldness will be the speedy answer to your petition.

But Hannah answered and said, "**No, my lord, I am a woman of sorrowful spirit. I have drunk neither wine nor intoxicating drink, but have poured out my soul before the Lord. 16 Do not consider your maidservant a wicked woman, for out of the abundance of my complaint and grief I have spoken until now.**"

Intercessory prayer with faith can quickly change one's physical and emotional state from grief and despair to expectant hope, as witnessed in Hannah's physical disposition after receiving the word from prophet Eli (v17-18).

Then Eli answered and said, "**Go in peace, and the God of Israel grant your petition which you have asked of Him.**" *And she said,* "**Let your maidservant find favor in your sight.**" *So the woman went her way and ate, and her face was no longer sad.*

Trust God amid every trial as you pray. Expect Him to provide the answer in a timely manner.

Action steps:

Can you a time you trusted God and offered Him dedicated prayer?

How did your outcome manifest?

What did you learn about God's character and faithfulness?

Give God thanks for every answered prayer.

In everything, choose to
Trust in the Lord with all your heart, and lean not on your own understanding; In all your ways acknowledge Him, and He shall direct your paths. (Proverbs 3:5-6)

Thought for Today

My guiding principle on prayer and intercession is:

Know prayer, know God;

How to receive God's victory:

Know God, know Victory;
No God, no victory.

The more we pray the greater our faith grows; the greater our faith the bigger mountains we can move with the Holy Spirit's backing. Commit to always give God the praise and honour for every victory He wins on your behalf.

Dr Jacqueline Samuels

How Often Should Christians Intercede?

My guiding principle on prayer and intercession is:
Know prayer, know God.
The same principle applies to receiving God's victory:
Know Prayer, know Victory. No prayer no victory.

The more we pray the greater our faith grows; the greater our faith the bigger mountains we can move with the Holy Spirit's backing. Commit to always give God the praise and honour for every victory He wins on your behalf.

But without faith it is impossible to please Him, for he who comes to God must believe that He is, and that He is a rewarder of those who diligently seek Him. (Hebrews 11:6)

The frequency of intercession can vary based on personal conviction, circumstances, and the Holy Spirit's leadership. No specific formula dictates how often Christians should intercede since prayer is a deeply personal and relational aspect of one's faith journey. However, here are some principles to consider:

Regular Communication: Just as healthy relationships thrive on regular communication, your relationship with God benefits from consistent prayer, including intercession.

Daily Prayer: Many Christians find it beneficial to incorporate intercession into their daily prayer routine. This can involve setting aside a specific time each day to pray for others and seek God's guidance.

Guided by the Holy Spirit: Allow the Holy Spirit to guide your intercessory prayers. If you feel prompted to pray for a specific person, situation, or need, respond to that prompting.

Variety and Depth: Intercession doesn't always need to be lengthy or intense. Short, heartfelt prayers throughout the day can complement more focused times of intercession.

Responding to Needs: Intercede as needs arise. When you hear about a situation or individual in need, take the opportunity to lift them up in prayer.

Seasons of Intensity: There might be seasons when you're led to dedicate more time to intercession due to significant needs or circumstances.

Balance and Rest: While intercession is important, remember that balance is key. Ensure that your commitment to intercession doesn't lead to burnout. Rest and self-care are also essential.

Personal Devotion: Intercession can be integrated into your personal devotional time, combining prayers for others with your own needs and reflections.

Group Prayer: Engage in group intercession through prayer meetings, small groups, or virtual communities. Group prayer adds diversity and collective strength to your intercessory efforts.

Listening Prayer: Practice listening prayer, where you spend time in silence, allowing God to reveal specific people or needs to pray for.

Flexibility: Be open to the Spirit's guidance. Sometimes, you might be called to intercede spontaneously, and other times you might have a specific list to work through.

Persistent Prayer: For certain situations or needs, persistent intercession can be powerful. Jesus encouraged persistent prayer in the parable of the persistent widow (Luke 18:1-8).

Ultimately, the frequency of intercession is a matter of your personal relationship with God. It's about cultivating a consistent and genuine connection with Him, where intercession becomes a natural outpouring of your love for others and your desire to partner with God in His work. Listen to His leading and find a rhythm of intercession that aligns with your spiritual journey.

Action steps:

What is your favourite time to commit to intercessory prayer?

What (if any) limitations to your prayer life can you identify?

How will you leverage your time to prioritize prayer in your life?

Do you currently belong to a prayer community? Yes / No

Is it online, in-person or both?

How will you avoid possible friction with your family as you guard your prayer time?

Why Intercede for Others

Christians are urged to intercede for other believers for several important reasons. Here are ten ways and reasons to intercede for others:

Obedience to Christ's Command:
Jesus taught the importance of loving one another and caring for each other. Intercessory prayer is a way to fulfill His command to love and support fellow believers.

Demonstrating Love and Unity:
Intercessory prayer demonstrates genuine love and unity within the body of Christ, showing that believers care for one another's spiritual and emotional well-being. James 5:16 encourages us to *pray for one another… The effective, fervent prayer of a righteous man avails much.*

Bearing One Another's Burdens:
Galatians 6:2 encourages believers to *bear one another's burdens and so fulfil the law of Christ*. Intercession helps lift the burdens of others and provides spiritual support during challenging times.

Strengthening the Faith of Others:
Intercessory prayer can uplift and strengthen the faith of fellow believers, reminding them of God's presence, love, and provision.

Spiritual Warfare:
Intercessory prayer engages in spiritual warfare, seeking God's protection and victory over spiritual battles that others may be facing.

Promoting God's Will:
By interceding for others, Christians align their prayers with God's will, asking for His purposes and plans to be fulfilled in the lives of fellow believers.

Fostering Gratitude and Thanksgiving:
Seeing prayers answered through intercession cultivates gratitude and encourages believers to give thanks to God for His faithfulness.

Building and Strengthening Relationships:
Regularly praying for others fosters a deeper sense of connection and care within the Christian community, building strong relationships.

Promoting Healing and Restoration:
Intercession can contribute to physical, emotional, and spiritual healing and restoration, as believers seek God's intervention in difficult situations.

Reflecting Christ's Character:
Intercessory prayer reflects the compassionate and merciful character of Christ, who intercedes on behalf of His followers before the Father.

Ultimately, intercession is a selfless act that reflects the heart of Christ and the deep bond that believers share as part of the body of Christ. It is a way to express love, empathy, and support, while also demonstrating trust in God's sovereignty and His ability to work in the lives of His people.

Action steps:

How does the instruction to *bear one another's burdens and so fulfil the law of Christ* (Galatians 6:2) apply to your prayer life?

Name 2 tips from the above list you would use to encourage a new believer who is struggling with building their prayer life.

Guide to Meditating on God's Word

Meditating on God's Word during intercession serves to deepen your connection with God, align your prayers with His will, and draw upon His wisdom and guidance as you intercede for others. Below are useful reasons why it's important and some tools, tips, and strategies for new intercessors:

Why we should meditate on God's Word during intercession

Alignment with God's Will: Meditating on Scripture helps you understand God's heart and purposes, ensuring your prayers are aligned with His desires for the situation.

Spiritual Insight: God's Word provides insight into the spiritual dynamics at play. Meditating on Scripture can reveal the spiritual root causes and solutions for the issues you're interceding about.

Authority in Prayer: Meditating on God's promises empowers your prayers with His authority. By speaking His Word, you declare His truth and power into the situation.

Strength and Encouragement: Scripture brings comfort, strength, and encouragement. Meditating on uplifting passages can sustain you as you intercede for challenging matters.

Spiritual Sensitivity: Regular meditation sensitizes you to the Holy Spirit's promptings and helps you discern how to pray effectively.

Growth and Transformation: Meditating on Scripture fosters personal growth, deepening your relationship with God and enhancing your intercessory skills.

14 Meditation tools and strategies for new intercessors

Select a Passage: Choose a Bible passage relevant to the situation you're interceding for. Focus on key verses that align with God's character and promises.

Create a Quiet Space: Find a quiet and comfortable place for meditation. Eliminate distractions to fully engage with God's Word.

Read and Reflect: Slowly read the selected passage. Reflect on its meaning, context, and implications for the situation you're praying about.

Repeat and Memorize: Repeat the passage to help internalize its message. Memorizing key verses enables you to recall them during intercession.

Pray Scripture: Turn the passage into a prayer. Incorporate its language and themes into your intercessory prayers.

Use Visualization: Imagine the situation being transformed according to the promises and principles in the passage. Visualize God's intervention.

Journaling: Write down insights, thoughts, and prayers inspired by the passage. Journaling helps solidify your understanding and keeps a record of your intercession.

Apply to Personal Life: Consider how the passage applies to your own life. Personal transformation enhances your effectiveness as an intercessor.

Pray with Others: Engage in group meditation and prayer. Discuss the passage and pray together for the situation.

Use Devotional Resources: Utilize devotionals, Bible study guides, and apps that focus on specific topics or themes for guided meditation.

Set Aside Time: Dedicate regular time for meditation. Consistency nurtures a habit of engaging with God's Word.

Listen to God: As you meditate, listen for God's promptings and insights. Be open to how He guides your prayers.

Start Small: Begin with shorter passages and gradually work your way to longer ones as you become more comfortable with meditation.

Be Patient: Meditation takes practice. Be patient with yourself as you grow in this spiritual discipline.

Remember that meditation is a journey of deepening your connection with God. As you incorporate Scripture into your intercession, you'll find your prayers becoming more effective, impactful, and aligned with God's heart and purposes.

Action steps:

Which of the above tools will you apply to further enrich your intercession?

Which five tools do you think are most beneficial for a new believer?

Pray and ask God to guide your decision making and action taking as you increase your intercessory skills going forward.

Commitment in Intercession

Do you sometimes feel like you don't have enough time to commit to daily prayer?

This is normal especially if your week consists of different activities, locations and schedules. Busy parents, students, professionals, ministry leaders all face the same time constraints in various seasons of life. This is why guarding and empowering your prayer life is essential for spiritual growth.

Remaining committed to intercession requires discipline, perseverance, and a strong sense of purpose.

Below are some useful tips to help you create a rhythm to stay committed in your intercessory prayer life:

Establish a Routine: Set a specific time and place for intercession each day. Consistency builds a habit and makes it easier to stay committed.

Set Realistic Goals: Start with achievable goals for the length and frequency of your intercession. Over time, you can gradually increase your commitment.

Stay Focused on Purpose: Remember why you started interceding in the first place. Keep your purpose and the impact of your prayers in mind.

Create a Prayer List: Maintain a list of people, situations, and topics you're interceding for. This keeps you organized and focused during your prayer time.

Use Prayer Tools: Utilize tools like journals, apps, or written prayers to guide and structure your intercession.

Journal Your Journey: Document your intercessory experiences, answered prayers, and insights. Reflecting on your journey can motivate you to stay committed.

Stay Connected to God's Word: Regularly read and meditate on Scripture. God's Word fuels your prayers and keeps your spiritual perspective clear.

Share with an Accountability Partner: Partner with a fellow believer who can hold you accountable and encourage you in your commitment to intercession.

Join a Prayer Group: Participate in a prayer group or community that supports and encourages one another in intercessory prayer.

Pray in Community: Praying with others, whether in person or virtually, can boost your commitment and provide fresh perspectives.

Celebrate Answered Prayers: When you see prayers being answered, take time to celebrate and give thanks. This reinforces the significance of your intercession.

Stay Open to God's Leading: Be flexible and open to the Holy Spirit's guidance during your prayer time. Let Him direct your prayers as needed.

Remind Yourself of the Impact: Remember that your intercession has a real impact on people's lives and spiritual battles. Your commitment matters.

Embrace the Process: Intercession is a journey. Embrace the ups and downs, knowing that growth and change take time.

Practice Self-Care: Take care of your physical, emotional, and spiritual well-being. When you're healthy, you're more likely to remain committed.

Stay Persistent in Challenges: Don't be discouraged by challenges or dry periods. Push through difficulties, knowing that they're a natural part of the journey.

Seek Encouragement: Reach out to mentors, leaders, or spiritual guides who can offer wisdom and encouragement in your intercessory journey.

Stay Grateful: Cultivate a heart of gratitude for the opportunity to intercede and partner with God in His work.

By implementing these tips, you'll be better equipped to maintain your commitment to intercession, and you'll experience the rewards of a deep and impactful prayer life.

Action steps:

Which of the above tips are you already doing? Acknowledge and take a moment to appreciate them below.

Which 5 tips will you do more of from the above list as you increase your commitment to prayer?

Chapter Five: TIME MANAGEMENT IN PRAYER

Time Management Tips for Intercession

Managing time effectively for prayer and intercession can be challenging, especially for busy individuals. However, with intentional planning and prioritization, it's possible to stay committed to your prayer life. Here are some time management tips to help you:

Prioritize Prayer:
Make prayer a non-negotiable priority in your daily schedule. Recognize its importance and allocate time for it just like you would for other important tasks.

Set Clear Goals:
Define specific prayer and intercession goals. Knowing what you're aiming for helps you allocate time accordingly.

Create a Prayer Schedule:
Set aside specific time slots for prayer and intercession each day. Consistency is key, so choose times when you're most alert and focused.

Use Small Time Windows:
Even if you have short breaks throughout the day, use them for quick prayers or moments of intercession. Every little bit counts.

Combine Prayer with Routine Tasks:
Pray while commuting, exercising, or doing household chores. This maximizes your time efficiency.

Limit Distractions:
During your designated prayer time, minimize distractions. Put away your phone and other potential interruptions.

Set Alarms or Reminders:
Use alarms or reminders to prompt you to pause and pray throughout the day.

Pray with Others:
Join or start a prayer group. Praying with others not only strengthens your commitment but also allows you to share the responsibility.

Pray in Transition:
Use transitions between tasks or activities as opportunities for brief prayers. This keeps your connection with God constant.

Batch Similar Tasks:
Group similar tasks together to create focused blocks of time for prayer and intercession.

Delegate or Outsource Tasks:
When possible, delegate tasks that others can handle, freeing up time for prayer and intercession.

Set Boundaries:
Establish clear boundaries with work, social commitments, and other activities to protect your prayer time.

Use Technology Wisely:
Use prayer apps, reminders, and digital tools to help you stay organized and on track.

Plan Prayer Retreats:
Occasionally set aside longer periods, such as a weekend, for focused prayer and intercession.

Reflect and Evaluate:
Regularly assess your time management strategies. Identify what's working well and where adjustments are needed.

Stay Flexible:
Be adaptable when unexpected events or tasks arise. Adjust your schedule but still find pockets of time for prayer.

Practice Gratitude:
Express gratitude to God for the time you have to connect with Him. A grateful mindset helps you appreciate and prioritize prayer.

Avoid Overcommitting:
Be mindful of your limits. Avoid taking on too many responsibilities that could crowd out your prayer time.

Remember that your commitment to prayer and intercession reflects your priorities and values. By intentionally managing your time, you can maintain a strong prayer life even amidst a busy schedule.

Intercession helps to Build Faith

Intercession is a powerful practice in the Christian faith that involves praying on behalf of others, lifting their needs, concerns, and requests to God. It not only builds the faith of those who are being prayed for but also strengthens the faith of those who engage in intercessory prayer. Here are ten key Bible verses that highlight the power of intercession and its role in building Christian faith:

Scriptures to Grow Faith with Intercession

James 5:16 - Confess your trespasses to one another, and pray for one another, that you may be healed. The effective, fervent prayer of a righteous man avails much.

1 Timothy 2:1-4 - Therefore I exhort first of all that supplications, prayers, intercessions, and giving of thanks be made for all men, for kings and all who are in authority, that we may lead a quiet and peaceable life in all godliness and reverence. For this is good and acceptable in the sight of God our Savior, who desires all men to be saved and to come to the knowledge of the truth.

Colossians 1:9-10 - For this reason we also, since the day we heard it, do not cease to pray for you, and to ask that you may be filled with the knowledge of His will in all wisdom and spiritual understanding; that you may walk worthy of the Lord, fully pleasing Him, being fruitful in every good work and increasing in the knowledge of God.

Romans 8:26-27 - Likewise the Spirit also helps in our weaknesses. For we do not know what we should pray for as we ought, but the Spirit Himself makes intercession for us with groanings which cannot be uttered. Now He who searches the hearts knows what the mind of the Spirit is, because He makes intercession for the saints according to the will of God.

1 Samuel 12:23 - Moreover, as for me, far be it from me that I should sin against the Lord in ceasing to pray for you; but I will teach you the good and the right way.

Ephesians 6:18 - Praying always with all prayer and supplication in the Spirit, being watchful to this end with all perseverance and supplication for all the saints.

Job 42:8 - Now therefore, take for yourselves seven bulls and seven rams, go to My servant Job, and offer up for yourselves a burnt offering; and My servant Job shall pray for you. For I will accept him, lest I deal with you according to your folly; because you have not spoken of Me what is right, as My servant Job has.

Philippians 1:3-4 - I thank my God upon every remembrance of you, always in every prayer of mine making request for you all with joy.

1 Thessalonians 5:17-18 - Pray without ceasing, in everything give thanks; for this is the will of God in Christ Jesus for you.

Numbers 6:24-26 - The Lord bless you and keep you; the Lord make His face shine upon you, and be gracious to you; the Lord lift up His countenance upon you, and give you peace.

Intercession plays a vital role in strengthening the bonds within the Christian community and building faith by expressing love, care, and empathy for one another. Through intercessory prayer, Christians demonstrate their reliance on God's power to bring about positive change and growth in the lives of others.

Action steps:

What are your favourite verses on prayer?
Write them below.

Thank God for His unfailing Word and remember to thank Him for every answered prayer.

Chapter Six: POWER OF SPIRITUAL WARFARE

Understanding Spiritual Warfare

Spiritual warfare refers to the battles that take place in the spiritual realm between the forces of good (God and His angels) and the forces of evil (Satan and his demonic forces). These battles can affect various aspects of our lives, including our thoughts, emotions, relationships, and spiritual well-being. Here are some of the main forms of spiritual warfare:

Temptation and Deception: Satan often tempts and deceives individuals to try and lead them away from God's truth and righteousness. This can involve tempting people with sinful desires, distorting God's Word, and leading them astray from their faith. Jesus taught us by example to always counter spiritual attacks with the Word of God.

Opposition to God's Work: When God is at work in individuals' lives or in communities, spiritual opposition can arise. This opposition may come in the form of obstacles, conflicts, or attacks meant to hinder God's purposes.

Attacks on Faith: Spiritual warfare can involve attacks on a believer's faith, causing doubt, confusion, and a sense of spiritual dryness. These attacks can challenge a person's trust in God and His promises. For instance: A person who is praying for physical healing and restoration may witness another receive their healing, while the one interceding doesn't receive it quickly. The enemy may then plant the seed of doubt aimed at diluting their prayerfulness.

Interference in Relationships: Demonic forces can seek to create division, strife, and misunderstanding within families, churches, and communities. This can lead to broken relationships and a weakening of unity.

Fear and Anxiety: Spiritual warfare can manifest as intense fear and anxiety, often fueled by negative thoughts and feelings that are not aligned with God's truth. The goal is to paralyze believers and prevent them from moving forward in their faith.

Physical and Emotional Attacks: While not always the case, some instances of physical and emotional distress may have spiritual warfare elements. Demonic forces can sometimes cause physical ailments, emotional turmoil, and other forms of suffering.

False Teachings and False Prophets: Satan and his agents may spread false teachings and doctrines that distort the truth of the Gospel and lead people away from God. This can happen within churches and religious communities.

Persecution: Persecution of Christians can also be a form of spiritual warfare. Hostility and violence directed toward believers can aim to silence their witness and undermine their faith.

Unforgiveness and Bitterness: Holding onto unforgiveness and bitterness can provide a foothold for spiritual attack, affecting a person's emotional and spiritual well-being.

Demonic Possession and Oppression: While relatively rare, some cases involve direct demonic possession or oppression, where individuals are under the control or influence of demonic entities.

Whenever we face spiritual attacks the believer's recourse is to stand in prayer and declare God's Word to counter every attack.

While spiritual warfare is real, believers have the tools and resources to stand against these attacks, outlined in Ephesians 6:10-18 below.

Finally, my brethren, **be strong in the Lord and in the power of His might. Put on the whole armor of God, that you may be able to stand against the wiles of the devil. For we** *do not* **wrestle** *against flesh and blood, but* **against principalities, against powers, against the rulers of the darkness of this age, against spiritual hosts of wickedness in the heavenly places. Therefore take up the whole armor of God, that you may be able to withstand in the evil day, and having done all, to stand.*

Stand therefore, having girded your waist with truth, having put on the breastplate of righteousness, and having shod your feet with the preparation of the gospel of peace; above all, taking the shield of faith with which you will be able to quench all the fiery darts of the wicked one. And take the helmet of salvation, and the sword of the Spirit, which is the word of God; <u>praying always with all prayer and supplication in the Spirit</u><u>,</u> *being watchful to this end with all perseverance and supplication for all the saints.* (Emphasis mine)

Spiritual warfare is about taking a stand against the powers of darkness. Anything that hinders our prayers from being answered must be uprooted in the Matchless Name of Jesus.

The Word of God is our greatest weapon. As we declare God's Word by faith He shows up and delivers us from every wicked plan of the enemy.

The armor of God described in Ephesians 6:10-18 above includes the *belt of truth*, the *breastplate of righteousness*, the *shoes of peace*, the *shield of faith*, the *helmet of salvation*, and the *sword of the Spirit* which is God's Word.

With these spiritual weapons, believers can resist and overcome the schemes of the enemy. Additionally, cultivating a strong prayer life, relying on God's Word, and seeking the Holy Spirit's guidance are three essential tools for navigating spiritual warfare.

How can believers apply the spiritual warfare weapons outlined in Ephesians 6:10-18?

The well-known passage uses the metaphor of armor to illustrate the spiritual tools and weapons that Christians are to employ in their battle against spiritual forces of darkness.

The passage emphasizes several key points about spiritual warfare and its meaning:

Identifying the Enemy: The passage makes it clear that the struggle is not merely against human opponents, but against spiritual forces of evil—*principalities, powers, rulers of darkness, and wicked spirits in heavenly places*. This indicates that there are unseen, malevolent forces at work in the spiritual realm.

Armor of God: Christians are urged to put on the "whole armor of God" to protect themselves and stand firm against the strategies and schemes of the devil. This armor includes:

- *Truth*: Represented as a belt, it signifies a commitment to honesty, integrity, and a firm foundation in God's Word.

- *Righteousness*: Portrayed as a breastplate, it symbolizes living a morally upright and godly life.

- *Gospel of Peace*: Reflected in footwear, it signifies readiness to share the message of peace and salvation.

- **Faith**: A shield that guards against doubts and attacks, highlighting the importance of unwavering trust in God.

- **Salvation**: A helmet protecting the mind, representing assurance of one's salvation.

Word of God: Described as a sword, it represents the power of Scripture in overcoming spiritual challenges.

Prayer and Supplication: The passage emphasizes the significance of constant prayer and supplication in the Spirit. This communication with God keeps believers connected to Him and helps them stay vigilant against spiritual threats.

Watchfulness and Perseverance: Christians are instructed to be watchful and perseverant, standing firm in their faith even when facing challenging circumstances.

The application of this passage involves recognizing the spiritual battles that believers face in their daily lives and being prepared to engage in them with *the armor of God*. It underscores the importance of aligning oneself with God's truth, righteousness, peace, faith, salvation, and the Word.

Regular prayer, reliance on God's strength, and an understanding of the spiritual realm are crucial elements to effectively engage in spiritual warfare.

Action steps:

Briefly describe what forms of spiritual warfare you have witnessed or engaged in.

Which spiritual armors will you ask God to empower in you to help you strengthen your prayer life?
Name them below then pray for endurance and deeper insight in the Matchless Name of Jesus.

🎯

🎯

🎯

🎯

🎯

🎯

Examples of Spiritual Warfare

Spiritual warfare can take various forms, and its manifestations can differ based on individual circumstances. Here are ten examples of spiritual warfare scenarios:

Temptation and Sin:
Example: A person struggles with an addiction and is constantly tempted to give in to their destructive habit. This battle involves resisting temptation and seeking God's strength to overcome sinful desire.

Struggles with Doubt and Faith:
Example: A believer faces a period of doubt and questions their faith. They wrestle with spiritual uncertainty and seek God's guidance to restore their trust in Him.

Attack on Relationships:
Example: A close-knit group of friends within a church community experiences conflicts and misunderstandings. The enemy seeks to disrupt their unity and harmony, prompting the need for reconciliation and prayer for healing.

Opposition to God's Calling:
Example: An individual feels a clear calling to a specific ministry or mission. As they step into this calling, they encounter unexpected challenges and resistance, requiring perseverance and reliance on God's strength.

Fear and Anxiety:
Example: A person suddenly experiences overwhelming fear and anxiety that seems to come out of nowhere. This attack targets their emotional well-being and trust in God's protection.

False Teaching and Deception:
Example: A charismatic leader emerges in a church, promoting teachings that deviate from the Bible's truth. This leader gains followers who are led astray by distorted doctrines.

Persecution and Hostility:
Example: A group of Christians in a restricted country faces persecution for their faith. They endure threats, imprisonment, and discrimination as they stand firm in their commitment to Christ.

Spiritual Dryness:
Example: A believer goes through a season of feeling distant from God. Their prayer and worship life feels dry and uninspired, prompting them to seek God's presence and renewal.

Unforgiveness and Bitterness:
Example: A person holds onto deep resentment and bitterness toward someone who has wronged them. This emotional burden becomes a foothold for spiritual attack, affecting their peace and spiritual growth.

Battle of the Mind:

Example: An individual struggles with persistent negative thoughts, self-doubt, and self-condemnation. These thoughts hinder their sense of worth and confidence in God's love.

It's important to remember that spiritual warfare is not always dramatic or overt. Sometimes, it manifests in subtle ways, such as planting doubts or negative thoughts. Prayer, reliance on God's Word, seeking godly counsel, and maintaining a strong relationship with God are crucial strategies in overcoming these challenges. Additionally, the support and intercession of fellow believers play a significant role in facing spiritual warfare.

Action steps:

What other examples of spiritual warfare do you know or practice? Name them below.

Intercessory Prayers for Spiritual Warfare

As you offer these intercessory prayers, remember that your role is to partner with God in spiritual warfare, calling upon His Strength and Authority to bring victory and freedom to those facing battles.

Prayer for Protection and Armor:
Heavenly Father, I intercede for those engaged in spiritual warfare. Clothe them with Your spiritual armor: *belt of truth, breastplate of righteousness, shoes of peace, shield of faith, helmet of salvation, and the sword of the Spirit*. May they stand strong against the schemes of the enemy, firmly rooted in Your Truth. In Jesus' Mighty Name, Amen.

Prayer for Strength in Battle:
Lord, I bring those facing spiritual battles before Your Throne of mercy. Strengthen their resolve and give them the courage to stand firm. Let Your power be their source of strength as they face the forces of darkness. Help them to overcome fear and doubt, relying on Your might. In the Matchless Name of Jesus I pray, Amen.

Prayer for Victory in Christ:
Gracious God, I pray for victory over the enemy's attacks. Remind everyone in spiritual warfare that they are more than conquerors through Christ who loves them. Grant them the assurance that no weapon formed against them shall prosper. May they experience Your triumphant power in every battle. In Jesus' Mighty Name, Amen.

Prayer for Discernment of Spiritual Warfare:
Heavenly Father, I intercede for discernment in recognizing spiritual warfare. Help Your children discern the subtle tactics of the enemy and distinguish between spiritual and earthly battles. Open their eyes to the schemes designed to hinder their faith and purpose. In Jesus' Name, Amen.

Prayer for Breaking Strongholds:
O Lord our Way Maker, I lift those facing strongholds and spiritual oppression. I ask You to break every chain and demolish every stronghold. Let Your light shine into the darkest areas of their lives, bringing freedom and healing. May they experience deliverance through Your mighty power. In the Matchless Name of Jesus, Amen.

Prayer for Covering and Blood of Jesus:
Gracious God, I cover every person engaged in spiritual warfare with the precious Blood of Jesus. Let Your Blood protect them from every attack and accusation of the enemy. May the Blood of Christ be their Shield and Refuge in times of battle. In Jesus' Glorious Name, Amen.

Prayer for Authority in Christ:
Heavenly Father, I intercede for those walking in the authority of Christ. Help them understand their identity in Christ and the power they have over demonic forces. Empower them to speak with authority and command every unclean spirit to flee. I ask this in Jesus' Powerful Name, Amen.

Prayer for Unity and Support:
Lord, I bring before You those engaging in spiritual warfare as a community. Strengthen their bonds of unity and support. Grant them the wisdom to stand together against the enemy's schemes. May their collective prayers and actions have a powerful impact on the spiritual realm. In the Precious Name of Jesus, Amen.

Prayer for God's Presence and Peace:
Gracious God, I pray for those in spiritual battles to experience Your abiding Presence and Peace. Let them rest in the assurance that You are with them. May Your Peace guard their hearts and minds in Christ Jesus as they face challenges. In Jesus' Name, Amen.

Prayer for Restoration and Healing:
Faithful Father, I intercede for restoration and healing for those wounded in spiritual warfare. Bind up their wounds and bring emotional, physical, and spiritual healing by Your Love. Restore what the enemy has stolen and replace it with Your abundant blessings. In the Mighty Name Jesus, Amen.

Action time:
Write your own warfare prayers below.

Chapter Seven: POWER OF SPIRITUAL DISCERNMENT

What is Spiritual Discernment?

Spiritual discernment is the ability to recognize and understand the spiritual influences and realities at play in every situation. It involves perceiving the difference between what is of God, what is of the enemy, and what may be human or worldly.

Spiritual discernment goes beyond mere intellectual understanding. I pray that as you develop a closer relationship with God you will become more sensitive to the Holy Spirit's guidance.

Spiritual Alertness for Effective Prayer

Becoming spiritually alert for effective prayer involves cultivating a deep connection with God, being attuned to the Holy Spirit's promptings, and growing to understand spiritual dynamics. Apply these steps to help you increase your spiritual alertness for effective prayer:

Develop a Strong Prayer Life:
Regular prayer deepens your relationship with God and opens your heart to receive His Divine guidance. Commit to spending time in both personal and communal prayer.

Study God's Word:
The Bible is a vital Source of spiritual wisdom and discernment. Study the Word of God regularly to understand His Truth and principles.

Practice Obedience:
Obedience to God's commands keeps you aligned with His will and helps you recognize His leading.

Cultivate Sensitivity to the Holy Spirit:
Purpose to commit time to commune with God. Spend time in silence and reflection, seeking the Holy Spirit's guidance and listening to His still, small Voice.

Be Aware of Your Thoughts and Emotions:
Pay attention to your thoughts and emotions. Are they aligned with God's Truth, or do they contradict His Word?

Stay Humble:
Humility opens you up to correction and guidance from God. Pride can blind you to spiritual truths. (Read 2 Chronicles 7:14; Psalm 25:9; 1 Peter 5:5-7, and Proverbs 22:4 to learn more about the importance of humility).

2 Chronicles 7:14 - *If My people who are called by My name will humble themselves, and pray and seek My face, and turn from their wicked ways, then I will hear from heaven, and will forgive their sin and heal their land.*

Psalm 25:9 - *The humble He guides in justice, and the humble He teaches His way.*

1 Peter 5:5-7. *Likewise you younger people, submit yourselves to your elders. Yes, all of you be submissive to one another, and be clothed with humility, for "**God resists the proud, but gives grace to the humble**." Therefore humble yourselves under the mighty hand of God, that He may exalt you in due time, casting all your care upon Him, for He cares for you.*

Proverbs 22:4 - *By humility and the fear of the Lord Are riches and honour and life.*

Surround Yourself with Godly Influences:
Engage with fellow believers who have strong discernment because their insights and experiences can be valuable.

Test the Spirits:
Evaluate teachings, ideas, and experiences against Scripture. Test the spirits to discern whether they are from God. As 1 John 4:1 advises, *Beloved, do not believe every spirit, but test the spirits, whether they are of God; because many false prophets have gone out into the world.*

Engage in Spiritual Warfare:
Recognize that spiritual battles are ongoing. *Put on the armor of God* (Ephesians 6:10-18) to stand against the enemy's schemes. (You can refer to the previous discussion on spiritual warfare).

Be Persistent in Prayer:
Persevere in prayer, seeking God's guidance and discernment over time. Sometimes, discernment unfolds gradually.

Seek God's Will Above Your Own:
Surrender your desires to God and seek His will above your own. This posture helps you align with His plans.

Stay Grounded in Love:
Love is a powerful force that helps you discern what is of God. Always evaluate situations through the lens of love and compassion.

Practice Fasting and Solitude:
Periods of fasting and solitude can enhance your spiritual sensitivity and connection with God.

Remember that spiritual discernment is a skill that grows over time. It requires humility, a willingness to learn, and a strong desire to draw closer to God. As you cultivate discernment, your prayers become more effective and aligned with God's heart and purposes.

In John 17:20-26 Jesus prayed for all believers:

"I do not pray for these alone, but also for those who will believe in Me through their word; that they all may be one, as You, Father, are in Me, and I in You; that they also may be one in Us, that the world may believe that You sent Me. **And the glory which You gave Me I have given them, that they may be one just as We are one: I in them, and You in Me; that they may be made perfect in one, and that the world may know that You have sent Me, and have loved them as You have loved Me.** *"Father, I desire that they also whom You gave Me may be with Me where I am, that they may behold My glory which You have given Me; for You loved Me before the foundation of the world.* **O righteous Father! The world has not known You, but I have known You; and these have known that You sent Me. And I have declared to them Your name, and will declare it, that the love with which You loved Me may be in them, and I in them.***"* (Emphasis mine)

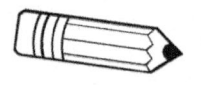

Action step:

As Jesus prayed for us, He has commissioned us to pray for the body of Christ around the world. Remember, someone prayed for you and me to know God through Jesus Christ. Let us now pay it forward by loving others through our prayers of intercession with discernment.

Discernment: Responding to God's Word

Responding to God's Word in the spirit of discernment involves understanding and applying the truths and messages found in Scripture with sensitivity to the leading of the Holy Spirit. Here's how you can approach responding to God's Word with a discerning heart:

Pray for Guidance: Before you read or study God's Word, pray for the Holy Spirit's guidance. Ask for wisdom, understanding, and discernment as you engage with the Scriptures.

Read Thoughtfully: As you read, take your time to understand the context, themes, and messages of the passage. Pay attention to details and nuances.

Listen to the Holy Spirit: Be open to the promptings of the Holy Spirit as you read. He can highlight specific verses or insights that apply to your life or situation.

Consider the Message's Application: Think about how the passage applies to your life. How does it align with your current circumstances, challenges, or decisions?

Compare with Other Scriptures: Check if the message aligns with other passages in the Bible. Discernment involves understanding Scripture as a whole.

Evaluate Motives and Attitudes: Discernment extends to your own motives and attitudes. Ask yourself whether your response is aligned with God's character and will.

Seek God's Confirmation: If a particular message resonates strongly, seek confirmation through prayer, further study, and seeking godly counsel.

Avoid Personal Bias: Be aware of your own biases and preferences that might influence your interpretation. Strive for an objective understanding.

Consider the Fruit: Evaluate whether the response aligns with the fruits of the Spirit described in Galatians 5:22-23. *But the fruit of the Spirit is love, joy, peace, longsuffering, kindness, goodness, faithfulness, gentleness, self-control. Against such there is no law.*

Seek Wise Counsel: If you're unsure about the interpretation or application of a passage, seek guidance from spiritually mature individuals or leaders.

Apply to Your Life: Once you've discerned the meaning and application of a passage, take intentional steps to apply it to your life. This might involve changes in behavior, attitudes, or priorities.

Pray for Transformation: Respond to God's Word with a prayer for transformation. Ask Him to work in your heart and enable you to live out the truths you've discerned.

Be Humble: Approach God's Word with humility, recognizing that your understanding is limited, and that God's wisdom is far greater.

Practice Regular Reflection: Reflect on how God's Word is shaping your thoughts, actions, and relationships over time. This ongoing process fosters discernment.

Continual Growth: Recognize that discernment is a skill that grows with experience and a deeper relationship with God. Keep seeking to grow in your ability to respond to His Word wisely.

Approaching God's Word with a spirit of discernment allows you to internalize its truths and apply them to your life in ways that align with God's will. It helps you avoid misunderstandings and ensures that your responses are rooted in truth and guided by the Holy Spirit.

Action time:

What are your *three priorities* in developing the spirit of discernment in your prayer life?

#1.

#2.

#3.

Write any additional insights below.

Discernment: Interpreting God's Word

Interpreting God's Word through spiritual discernment involves understanding Scripture with the guidance of the Holy Spirit, aiming to uncover its deeper meanings and applications. Here's a step-by-step approach to interpreting the Bible with spiritual discernment:

Prayerful Approach:
Begin with prayer, asking the Holy Spirit to guide you as you read and interpret the Scriptures. Invite Him to open your heart and mind to understand God's message.

Study the Context:
Understand the historical, cultural, and literary context of the passage. Consider who the author and original audience were, the time period, and the purpose of the writing.

Read the Whole Passage:
Read the entire passage before focusing on specific verses. This helps you grasp the passage's overall message and prevents taking verses out of context.

Listen to the Spirit:
As you read, be attentive to any insights or promptings from the Holy Spirit. He may highlight certain verses or themes that are relevant to your current situation.

Use Cross-References:
Refer to other parts of the Bible that relate to the passage you're studying. Cross-references can provide a broader understanding of the topic.

Examine Key Words and Themes:
Identify keywords and recurring themes in the passage. Consider their meanings and significance within the context.

Understand the Original Language:
If possible, explore the original Hebrew or Greek words used in the passage. This can provide deeper insights into the text's nuances.

Reflect and Apply:
Consider how the passage applies to your life. What truths or principles can you glean from it? How can you live out its message?

Seek Balance:
Discernment involves finding a balanced interpretation that aligns with the entirety of Scripture. Avoid interpretations that contradict clear biblical teachings.

Check with Sound Theology:
Ensure your interpretation is consistent with sound theological principles and aligns with the character of God.

Consult Commentaries and Resources:
Use reputable commentaries, Bible dictionaries, and study resources to gain additional insights from scholars and theologians.

Test with Personal Application:
Apply the insights you've gained from the passage to your own life. Test whether they lead to personal growth, transformation, and alignment with God's will.

Discuss with Others:
Engage in discussions with fellow believers or mentors who can offer diverse perspectives and insights.

Wait and Reflect:
Sometimes, insights may come to you gradually. Allow time for reflection and further study as you continue to seek understanding.

Apply Humility:
Approach Scripture with humility, recognizing that our understanding is limited. Be open to correction and growth in your interpretations.

Trust the Holy Spirit's Guidance:
Ultimately, trust that the Holy Spirit is the ultimate Teacher and Guide. Rely on His wisdom and guidance as you interpret God's Word.

Interpreting God's Word through spiritual discernment is a dynamic process that requires an ongoing relationship with God and a willingness to learn and grow in your understanding. It's a journey that deepens your knowledge of God's truth and transforms your life as you apply His teachings.

Action time:

Which of these strategies will start to apply today?

Verses on the Spirit of Discernment

The following verses highlight the value of discernment as the ability to:

- differentiate between truth and falsehood
- understand God's will, and
- make wise judgments based on the guidance of the Holy Spirit and the Word of God.

Take a few moments to prayerfully read the following verses relating to the spirit of discernment and ask the Holy Spirit to reveal His secrets to you.

Proverbs 2:3-6 - *Yes, if you cry out for discernment, and lift up your voice for understanding, if you seek her as silver, and search for her as for hidden treasures; then you will understand the fear of the Lord, and find the knowledge of God. For the Lord gives wisdom; from His mouth come knowledge and understanding.*

1 Corinthians 2:14-16 - *But the natural man does not receive the things of the Spirit of God, for they are foolishness to him; nor can he know them, because they are spiritually discerned. But he who is spiritual judges all things, yet he himself is rightly judged by no one. For "who has known the mind of the Lord that he may instruct Him?" But we have the mind of Christ.*

1 John 4:1 - *Beloved, do not believe every spirit, but test the spirits, whether they are of God; because many false prophets have gone out into the world.*

Hebrews 4:12 - *For the Word of God is living and powerful, and sharper than any two-edged sword, piercing even to the division of soul and spirit, and of joints and marrow, and is a discerner of the thoughts and intents of the heart.*

Philippians 1:9-10 - *And this I pray, that your love may abound still more and more in knowledge and all discernment, that you may approve the things that are excellent, that you may be sincere and without offense till the day of Christ.*

Romans 12:2 - *And do not be conformed to this world, but be transformed by the renewing of your mind, that you may prove what is that good and acceptable and perfect will of God.*

James 1:5 - *If any of you lacks wisdom, let him ask of God, who gives to all liberally and without reproach, and it will be given to him.*

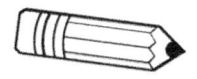

Action time:

Do you know any other verses on discernment? Add them below.

Hot Tip: The more you apply the Word in your prayer life, the more impact you will experience, to the glory of God the Father.

Intercessory Prayers for Spiritual Discernment

Use the following intercessory prayers as a foundation as you pray for spiritual discernment and purpose:

Prayer for Spiritual Discernment:
Heavenly Father, I come before You on behalf of those seeking spiritual discernment. Grant them wisdom, insight, and a sensitive heart to perceive Your guidance amidst life's complexities. Illuminate their minds with the light of Your Truth, that they may distinguish between Your Voice and the world's distractions. May their discernment lead to wise decisions and a deeper intimacy with You. In Jesus' Matchless Name, Amen.

Prayer for Clarity of Purpose:
Lord, I intercede for those longing for clarity in their life's purpose. Open their hearts to receive Your Divine revelation and insight. Help them recognize their unique calling and how their gifts align with Your kingdom agenda. May they experience a deep sense of purpose that propels them forward with passion and confidence. In the Powerful Name of Jesus, Amen.

Prayer for Surrendered Hearts:
Gracious God, I pray for those desiring to surrender their lives fully to Your purposes. Teach them to yield their plans, ambitions, and desires to You. May they find peace in letting go of their own agendas and embracing Your Divine will. Grant them the humility to trust Your plans, even when the path is unclear. In the Mighty Name of Jesus, Amen.

Prayer for Discerning God's Will:
Heavenly Father, I uplift those seeking to discern Your will for their lives. Guide them as they search for direction and seek Your guidance. Give them patience as they wait on You for answers. May they have confidence that as they seek Your will, You will reveal the steps they should take. Empower them to daily walk obediently with faith. In Jesus' Precious Name, Amen.

Prayer for Holistic Discernment:
Lord, I intercede for those needing discernment in every area of their lives. Help them discern not only spiritual matters but also relationships, decisions, and priorities. Grant them the ability to see beyond the surface and perceive the underlying spiritual dynamics. May their discernment lead to a balanced and purposeful life. In the Mighty Name of Jesus, Amen.

Prayer for Discernment in Relationships:
Gracious God, I pray for discernment in relationships. Guide those seeking godly connections and partnerships. Help them recognize those who will support their spiritual growth and purpose. Protect them from relationships that could hinder their journey. May their discernment lead to mutually beneficial relationships that honour God. In Jesus' Matchless Name, Amen.

Prayer for Strength in Discernment:
Heavenly Father, I bring to You those facing challenges in their pursuit of discernment and purpose. Grant them strength and resilience. Help them trust in Your provision and guidance, even when the way seems unclear. May they draw on Your strength to navigate challenges and emerge with deeper faith and clearer purpose. In Jesus' Mighty Name, Amen.

Prayer for Divine Revelation:
Lord, I intercede for Divine revelation in the lives of those seeking purpose and discernment. Open their eyes to hidden truths and insights found in Your Word. Illuminate their understanding of Your plans for them. May they encounter revelations that transform their perspectives and propel them into their God-given purpose. In the Name of Jesus, Amen.

As you raise these intercessory prayers before the LORD, allow the Holy Spirit to guide your words and intercede on behalf of those seeking spiritual discernment and purpose.

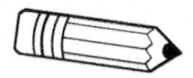

Action time:

What are your new prayers for spiritual discernment and purpose? Write them below.

Chapter Eight: POWER OF SPIRITUAL INTEGRITY

What is Spiritual Integrity?

Spiritual integrity refers to the alignment between a person's inner values, beliefs, and character with their outward actions and behavior. It involves living consistently with one's deeply held spiritual convictions and maintaining a strong moral compass based on their faith and relationship with God.

Importance of Maintaining Spiritual Growth and Integrity

Whatever we do not nurture dies. John 15:5 declares: *I am the vine, you are the branches.* **He who abides in Me, and I in him, bears much fruit; for without Me you can do nothing.** Growing in faith and integrity yields consistent results and keeps us connected to Jesus Christ the Vine.

Here are fifteen reasons why spiritual integrity is crucial to a believer's growth:

Honour to God: Spiritual integrity reflects a believer's commitment to honouring God in all aspects of life. It's a way to bring glory to God by living in accordance with His teachings revealed through His Word.

Authentic Witness: Believers are called to be witnesses of Christ's love and truth. Spiritual integrity ensures that their actions match their words, making their witness credible and impactful.

Personal Growth: Living with integrity encourages personal growth and transformation. It prompts believers to address areas of weakness and sin, leading to spiritual maturity.

Consistency: Spiritual integrity fosters consistency between one's public and private life. This consistency builds trust and credibility among peers and society.

Relational Health: Integrity fosters healthy relationships built on trust and honesty. It prevents deception and hypocrisy that can damage relationships.

Effective Ministry: Spiritual leaders with integrity have a more significant impact on their followers. Their actions and teachings are aligned, making their ministry more effective.

Resilience in Trials: A person with spiritual integrity is more likely to stand firm in their faith during trials and challenges. Their unwavering commitment to their beliefs provides strength.

A Clear Conscience: Walking in integrity leads to a clear conscience before God and others. This inner peace contributes to emotional and mental well-being.

Avoiding Hypocrisy: Jesus strongly criticized hypocrisy. Spiritual integrity helps believers avoid the pitfalls of hypocrisy by living transparently.

Honour God's Standards: Spiritual integrity involves upholding God's moral standards, even when faced with worldly pressure or temptations.

Avoiding Compromise: Believers with spiritual integrity are less likely to compromise their values for personal gain or approval from others.

Reflecting Christ's Character: Spiritual integrity reflects Christ's character of truth, love, and righteousness. It allows believers to emulate His example.

Guided by the Holy Spirit: Maintaining spiritual integrity involves relying on the guidance of the Holy Spirit to discern right from wrong and make godly choices.

Stewardship of Influence: Those in leadership positions have a responsibility to model integrity, as their actions influence others' faith and behavior.

Eternal Perspective: Spiritual integrity keeps believers focused on eternal values rather than temporary gain or pleasure.

In summary, spiritual integrity is vital to a believer's identity, growth, and witness. It aligns their lives with their faith and allows them to embody Christ's teachings and character in a world that often lacks consistency and authenticity.

Develop Spiritual Integrity for Godly Purpose

Developing spiritual integrity to fulfill a godly purpose involves aligning your character and actions with God's principles and values. Follow these steps to cultivate spiritual integrity and live out your purpose:

Know God's Word:
Study and meditate on the Bible to understand God's truths and principles. Let His Word guide your thoughts, decisions, and actions.

Pray Regularly:
Develop a consistent prayer life to seek God's guidance, wisdom, and strength in pursuing your purpose.

Align with God's Will:
Seek to discern God's will for your life. Surrender your desires to His plans and submit to His leadership.

Practice Honesty and Transparency:
Be truthful in all your interactions and dealings. Avoid deception or manipulation in your words and actions.

Live with Integrity in All Areas:
Display consistency between your public and private life. Let your character shine through in every situation.

Admit Mistakes and Seek Forgiveness:
When you make a mistake, acknowledge it, seek forgiveness from God and others involved, and learn from the experience.

Cultivate Humility:
Recognize your limitations and dependence on God. Avoid pride and arrogance and purpose to always treat others with respect and humility.

Guard Your Heart and Mind:
Protect your mind from negative influences, temptations, and ungodly thoughts. Fill your thoughts with things that are true, noble, and pure (Philippians 4:8).

Practice Generosity and Compassion:
Show love and compassion to others, reflecting Christ's character in your thoughts, intentions, actions and interactions.

Be Accountable:
Surround yourself with trustworthy mentors, friends, or spiritual advisors who can hold you accountable and offer guidance. Your character is frequently influenced by the five people you spend the most time with. If your closest friends are creating a toxic atmosphere around you, find a way to minimize the time you spend in their presence.

Resist Peer Pressure and Worldly Influences:
Stand firm in your convictions even when facing pressure to compromise your integrity. Protect your spiritual space.

Examine Your Motives:
Regularly assess your motives for your actions. Ensure they align with serving God's purposes rather than seeking personal gain or recognition.

Practice Forgiveness:
Forgive those who have wronged you and release any bitterness or resentment. This helps maintain a heart of integrity.

Practice Obedience:
Obey God's commands even when it's challenging. Your obedience is an expression of your integrity.

Seek Growth and Transformation:
Continuously strive for spiritual growth and transformation. Allow the Holy Spirit to work within you to refine your character.

Persevere through Challenges:
Expect challenges and obstacles as you pursue your godly purpose. Persevere with faith and integrity, trusting God's faithfulness.

Reflect and Evaluate:
Regularly reflect on your actions and decisions. Evaluate whether they align with your purpose and God's standards.

Developing spiritual integrity is a lifelong journey. It requires a commitment to growing in your relationship with God and intentionally living out His values. As you prioritize integrity, you'll find yourself better equipped to fulfill your godly purpose and bring honour to God in all you do.

Verses Celebrating Integrity

Applying integrity involves **walking in honesty, righteousness, and truthfulness in all aspects of life**. It means being consistent and transparent, even when no one is watching. Integrity guides our decisions, actions, and interactions with others. Walking in integrity reflects our relationship with God and our commitment to living according to His standards.

Read, meditate on and apply the following Bible verses on integrity.

Proverbs 10:9 - *He who walks with integrity walks securely, but he who perverts his ways will become known.*

Proverbs 11:3 - *The integrity of the upright will guide them, but the perversity of the unfaithful will destroy them.*

Psalm 25:21 - *Let integrity and uprightness preserve me, for I wait for You.*

Psalm 26:1 - *Vindicate me, O Lord, for I have walked in my integrity. I have also trusted in the Lord; I shall not slip.*

Proverbs 20:7 - *The righteous man walks in his integrity; his children are blessed after him.*

Micah 6:8 - *He has shown you, O man, what is good; and what does the Lord require of you but to do justly, to love mercy, and to walk humbly with your God?*

Proverbs 28:6 - *Better is the poor who walks in his integrity than one perverse in his ways, though he be rich.*

Psalm 15:1-2 - *Lord, who may abide in Your tabernacle? Who may dwell in Your holy hill? He who walks uprightly, and works righteousness, and speaks the truth in his heart.*

2 Corinthians 8:21 - *Providing honourable things, not only in the sight of the Lord, but also in the sight of men.*

Ephesians 6:14 - *Stand therefore, having girded your waist with truth, having put on the breastplate of righteousness.*

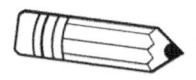

Action time:

Write 3-5 prayer points based on the above Scriptures.

Intercessory Prayers for Spiritual Integrity

You can use the following intercessory prayers as a starting point to pray for spiritual integrity and purpose. Remember, you can add the names of specific people the Holy Spirit brings to your mind.

Prayer for Personal Integrity:
Heavenly Father, I bring those who are seeking to live with spiritual integrity before You. May they be guided by Your Word and empowered by Your Spirit to walk in honesty, transparency, and righteousness. Protect them from the snares of hypocrisy and grant them the strength to stand firm in their convictions. Help them to live out their faith with authenticity and honour, in Jesus' Matchless Name, Amen.

Prayer for Clear Purpose:
Lord, I intercede for those who are seeking clarity in their purpose. Please reveal Your plan for their lives and give them a sense of direction. Help them understand how their unique gifts and talents align with Your Kingdom purposes. May they be steadfast in pursuing Your will, even in the face of uncertainty. Guide them to fulfill the purposes You have ordained for them. In the Mighty Name of Jesus, Amen.

Prayer for Consistent Devotion:
Gracious God, I pray for those striving to maintain consistent devotion to You. Grant them the discipline and desire to spend time in prayer, studying Your Word, and seeking Your Presence. Strengthen their commitment to seek You above all else and deepen their relationship with You. May their devotion lead to spiritual growth, transformation, and a deeper understanding of Your purposes. In Jesus' Matchless Name, Amen.

Prayer for Wisdom and Discernment:
Heavenly Father, I lift to You all who are seeking wisdom and discernment as they navigate their paths. Grant them the ability to discern between Your will and the world's distractions. Fill them with Your Holy Spirit, that they may make choices aligned with Your Word and guided by Your wisdom. May their pursuit of spiritual integrity and purpose be marked by discerning hearts. In Jesus' Name, Amen.

Prayer for Alignment with God's Will:
Lord, I intercede for those desiring to align their lives with Your will. Help them surrender their plans and desires to You, yielding to Your perfect purposes. Give them the courage to let go of their own agendas and trust in Your Divine guidance. May their commitment to living in alignment with Your will bring them true fulfillment and spiritual integrity, in the Name of Jesus, Amen.

Prayer for Strength in Adversity:
Gracious God, I pray for those facing challenges and adversity as they pursue spiritual integrity and purpose. Strengthen them with Your grace and resilience. May their faith remain unwavering, and may they find solace in Your Presence during difficult times.

Grant them the perseverance to press on, knowing that You are their ultimate Source of strength in Jesus' Mighty Name, Amen.

Prayer for Impactful Purpose:
Heavenly Father, I lift to You those seeking to live impactful purposes in their lives. Bless them with opportunities to make a positive difference in the lives of others. Use their gifts, passions, and experiences to bring glory to Your Name. May their pursuit of purpose be a testimony of Your transformative work and a beacon of light to those around them, in the Matchless Name of Jesus, Amen.

As you intercede for spiritual integrity and purpose, remember to personalize these prayers and allow the Holy Spirit to guide your words and intentions.

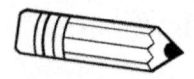

Action time:

Write down prayers for those the Holy Spirit brings to your mind.

As you continually pray for others, God will answer your faith-based prayers and commitment.

Conclusion

Continual intercession with integrity, discipline, and commitment is a powerful and transformative practice that reflects your deep relationship with God and your dedication to serving others. Here are some final thoughts to encourage you in your journey of intercession:

Integrity Matters: Enhance your commitment to intercession by maintaining integrity in your motives, actions, and prayers. Let your intercession be marked by sincerity and alignment with God's will.

Discipline Yields Fruit: Consistent discipline in intercession yields fruit over time. Just as physical training requires consistent effort, your commitment to prayer will bear spiritual fruit and impact lives.

Leading by Example: By committing to intercession, you will set an example for others to follow. Your prayers can inspire and encourage those around you to engage more deeply in their own prayer lives.

Spiritual Growth: Intercession with integrity, discipline, and commitment will boost your own spiritual growth. You will draw closer to God and foster a deeper understanding of His heart and purposes.

Effectiveness in Prayer: Intentional and committed intercession has the potential to bring about powerful changes in individuals, situations, and even nations. Your prayers matter and make a difference, so don't hold back the gift of prayer and intercession the LORD has instilled in you.

Lifting Others Up: Intercession is a way to selflessly uplift the needs of others before God. It's an expression of love, compassion, and empathy for those who need God's intervention. The more you pray for others, the deeper revelations you will receive; you will empower more people.

Fellowship with God: As you commit to intercession, you experience a unique fellowship with God. You partner with Him in His work and become a conduit for His grace and mercy.

Overcoming Challenges: In your commitment to intercession, you will face challenges and distractions. Stay steadfast in your discipline and trust that God is working through your prayers. He will always stand by His Word.

A Lifelong Journey: Intercession is not a one-time task but a lifelong journey. Cultivate the discipline and commitment that will sustain you for the long haul.

Balancing Grace and Effort: While discipline and commitment are important, remember that your intercession is ultimately a response to God's grace. It is important to balance your efforts with relying on His strength.

Leave Room for Rest: Even in your commitment, remember to rest and recharge. Balance your intercessory efforts with times of personal reflection, relaxation, and Sabbath rest.

Celebrate Victories: Celebrate answered prayers and the positive impacts of your intercession. Let these successes fuel your commitment and passion.

Remain Humble: Remain humble in your role as an intercessor. Recognize that you are a vessel through which God will accomplish His work.

Trust God's Timing: Not all answers to prayer will be immediate or evident. Trust that God's timing is perfect and that He is working according to His Sovereign plan.

Persevere in Adversity: Commitment to intercession may be tested during difficult times. Continue to intercede even when circumstances seem challenging. The God of abounding Grace is always with you.

Stay Focused on God: Let your commitment to intercession draw you closer to God Himself. Keep Him at the center of your efforts and continually rely on His wisdom and guidance.

Intercession with integrity, discipline, and commitment is a sacred privilege and responsibility. It is an invitation to partner with God in His redemptive work, and an opportunity to impact lives through the power of prayer. As you continue along this journey, may you experience the joy and fulfillment that come from interceding with a heart aligned with God's purposes.

Finally,

But may the God of all grace, who called us to His eternal glory by Christ Jesus, *after you have suffered a while,* **perfect, establish, strengthen, and settle you.** (1 Peter 5:10)

Bible Verse

1 Peter 5:10 (NKJV)

But may the God of all grace, who called us to His eternal glory by Christ Jesus, after you have suffered a while, perfect, establish, strengthen, and settle you.

upon **GRACE GRACE**

About the Author

Dr Jacqueline Njeri Samuels has devoted her life to serving her gifts to help thousands of creative superstars confidently show up and shine in their strengths.

A book publisher, graphic designer, qualified life coach and educator with a PhD in Music and SEN from Reading University UK, the author is a wife and mother, songwriter and Gospel artist. She believes we are all blessed with gifts we can share to help heal the world.

Dr Jackie has won numerous awards, trophies, and certificates of achievement from Kenya, South Africa, France and the UK in recognition of her commitment to empower others in music, mentorship, education and more.

The author is an ordained Pastor and the Global Worship Coordinator for *Supreme Global Outreach (SGO)*, a registered Charity in the UK and Zambia whose mission is to support and empower the less fortunate. Pastor Jackie has travelled severally to Zambia on missions with SGO's Founder and President Chaplain Elizabeth Simuchimba.

The cathartic writing process of her first book *'Push Through: Release Your Past and Step Into Your Divine Destiny'* in 2018 unlocked Pastor Jackie's restoration from trauma and aligned her life's purpose. She is committed to helping creatives publish instructional and self-help resources for individuals of all ages.

Training courses and products are available at:
https://serve-and-thrive-academy.thinkific.com/

Follow the Author on Amazon to be notified of new releases.
https://www.amazon.com/author/jacquelinensamuels

Connect with the Author

Other books by the Author are available at:
https://www.amazon.com/author/jacquelinensamuels
UK: https://tinyurl.com/AuthorJNSamuelsUK

Join us for weekly prayer, thanksgiving, and worship at Supreme Global Outreach:
FB: https://tinyurl.com/SupremeGlobalOutreachFB
IG: https://www.instagram.com/supremeglobaloutreach/
TikTok: https://www.tiktok.com/@supremeglobaloutr

Has this book blessed you? <u>Please Follow us on Amazon</u> and leave your best 5* review.
Share this book's **ISBN: 9798858994800** with your friends who need a spiritual breakthrough. May God reward your efforts.
https://www.amazon.com/author/jacquelinensamuels

Other resources include:
- Prayer books for adults and children
- Educational material for children and young adults,
- Colouring Bible verse books for children and teens,
- Colouring books for adults to create calm mindfulness.

To access more self-study resources, go to:
https://tinyurl.com/ServeAndThrive

Thanks for connecting,
Looking forward to reading your reviews and testimonies.
Thank you, Superstar!
God continually bless and refresh you!
Dr Jackie

Power of Intercession

Check out some of the books by Dr Jacqueline Samuels in the **Serve &Thrive** and **Creative Mindfulness** series available on Amazon.

Visit Amazon for more in the *Serve and Thrive* and *Creative Mindfulness* book Series.

https://tinyurl.com/AuthorJNSamuelsUK

Some Children's and YA educational books:
https://tinyurl.com/AuthorJNSamuelsUK

Discover how to self-publish your books:
https://serve-and-thrive-academy.thinkific.com/

Download Your Gratitude Starter Kit — DOWNLOAD

https://tinyurl.com/GratitudeStarterKit1

Printed in Great Britain
by Amazon